Spotter's Guide to

MOTORBIKES

World road bikes since 1975

David Minton

Designed by Kim Blundell
Edited by Helen Davies

Contents

Photographs provided by Doug Jackson, Martyn Barnwell, *Which Bike?*, *Motorcycle Weekly* and motorbike manufacturers.
Illustrations by Tony Gibbons, Clive Spong, Dee McLean Graham Smith and Kim Blundell

First published in 1980 by Usborne Publishing Ltd, 20 Garrick Street, London WC2E 9BJ, England.

Published in Australia by Rigby Publishing Ltd, Adelaide, Sydney, Melbourne, Brisbane.

GRAFICAS REUNIDAS, S. A.
Av. de Aragón, 56 — Madrid-27.

How to use this book

This book is an identification guide to motorbikes. There are photographs of over 80 bikes made between 1975 and 1979 with their special points marked to help you recognize them.

All the bikes of one make are grouped together and the makes are arranged alphabetically by the name of the manufacturer. The bikes are from all over the world and nearly all of them are road bikes, that is, bikes for normal road riding.

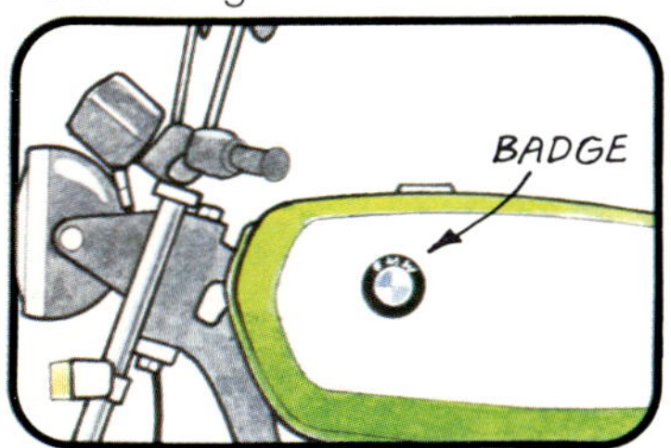

When you spot a bike, first find out what make it is. Look for the name of the manufacturer which is usually painted on the petrol tank or side of the bike. Then look in the contents list on the left and find the pages for that manufacturer.

To work out which bike it is, look for the model name or number on the bike. Look, too, at the shape of the engine and how the cylinders are arranged. On page 4 you can find out how to recognize the different types of engine. Check the other parts of the bike are the same, too.

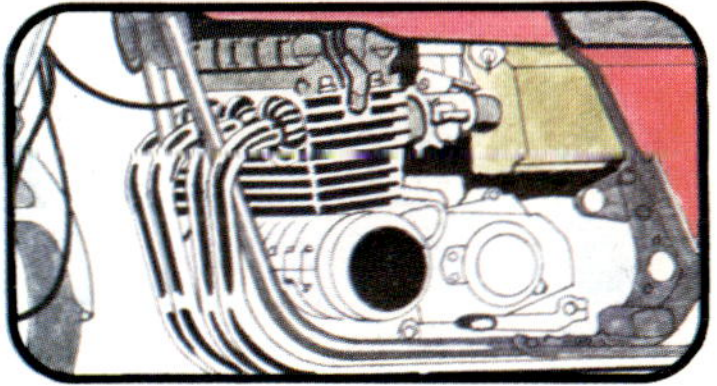

Some bike owners fix special seats and handlebars to their bikes and these may make them look a bit different from the pictures. You can see some of these accessories on page 49. You may also spot some off-road bikes which are specially built for racing or cross-country riding. There are some pictures of these on pages 50–52.

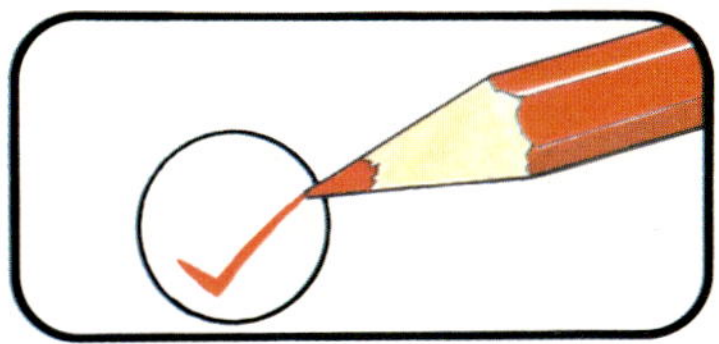

Each time you spot a bike, you can tick the circle near the picture of that bike. You can keep a record of all the bikes you spot in the scorecard.

Hints on motorbike spotting

A good way to recognize a motorbike is by looking at its engine. The engine may have between one and six cylinders and the pictures below show the various ways that the cylinders can be arranged. The number of exhaust pipes from the engine usually shows how many cylinders there are. The volume of all the cylinders together gives the engine size, which is measured in cubic centimetres (cc). The engine's power is measured in brake horse power (bhp). A motorbike with a single-cylinder engine is often called a "single", and one with a three-cylinder engine a "triple", and so on.

Types of engine

Single
Engine with one cylinder and usually one exhaust pipe.

Parallel twin
Two cylinders placed side-by-side across the bike.

Flat twin
Two cylinders placed end-to-end across the bike.

In-line V-twin
Two cylinders placed along the bike in a V-shape.

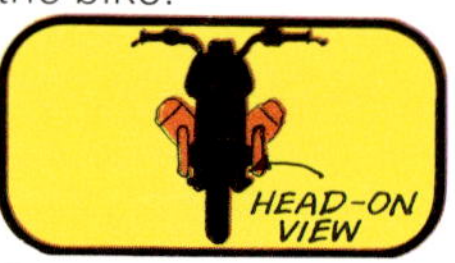

Transverse V-twin
Two cylinders placed across the bike in a V-shape.

Triple
Three cylinders side-by-side across the bike.

Transverse four
Four cylinders placed side-by-side across the bike.

Flat four
Four cylinders lying in pairs, end-to-end across the bike.

Six
Six cylinders placed side-by-side across the bike.

Engine noises

Engines may be two-stroke or four-stroke. Two-stroke engines have a high-pitched, buzzing sound like a lawnmower. Four-stroke engines make a deeper, slower noise.

Types of bike

Here are the main types of bikes in this book. They can be identified by their shape and by the number and position of the cylinders in the engine.

Moped
Engine of 50cc or less and top speed of 50kph. Usually single cylinder.

Scooter
Low, step-through body, small wheels, leg shields and cover over engine.

Commuter
Small bike with engine usually under 200cc and few accessories.

Sportster
Built for speed with high-powered engine, strong brakes and low handlebars.

Tourer
Bike for long-distance riding with large petrol tank, big seat and space for luggage.

Trail bike*
On- or off-road bike with heavy tread "trials" tyres, high-level exhaust system and high mudguards so mud does not clog the wheels.

Parts of a bike

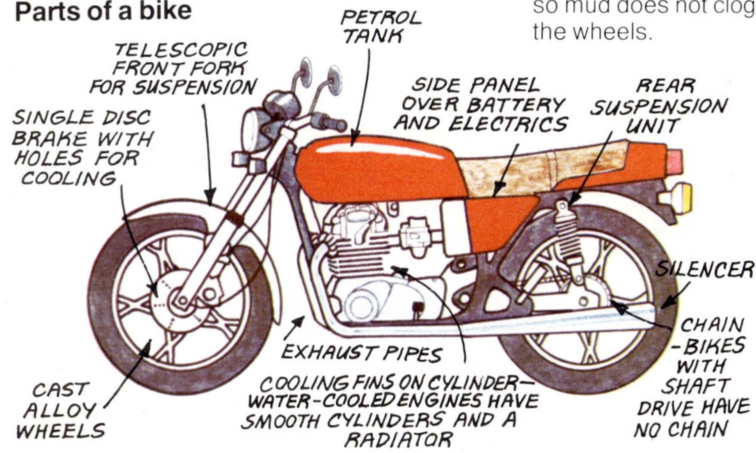

*Trail bikes look similar to trials and enduro bikes (see pages 50–51) but are not built for riding in competitions.

AJS (U.K.), Batavus (Netherlands)

▼AJS FB Ajay
An old-fashioned, but beautifully made trail bike. It has a four-speed gearbox and single-cylinder, two-stroke, 247cc engine.

Batavus Starglo 2▲
Single-speed moped with 48cc, single-cylinder, two-stroke engine and top speed of 50kph. Batavus is one of the biggest moped factories in Holland, which is the world's top moped manufacturing country.

Benelli (Italy)

▼Benelli 254
Small, lightweight sportster which has 231cc, four-stroke, four-cylinder engine giving 28bhp and a top speed of 150kph. It has a five-speed gearbox and powerful brakes.

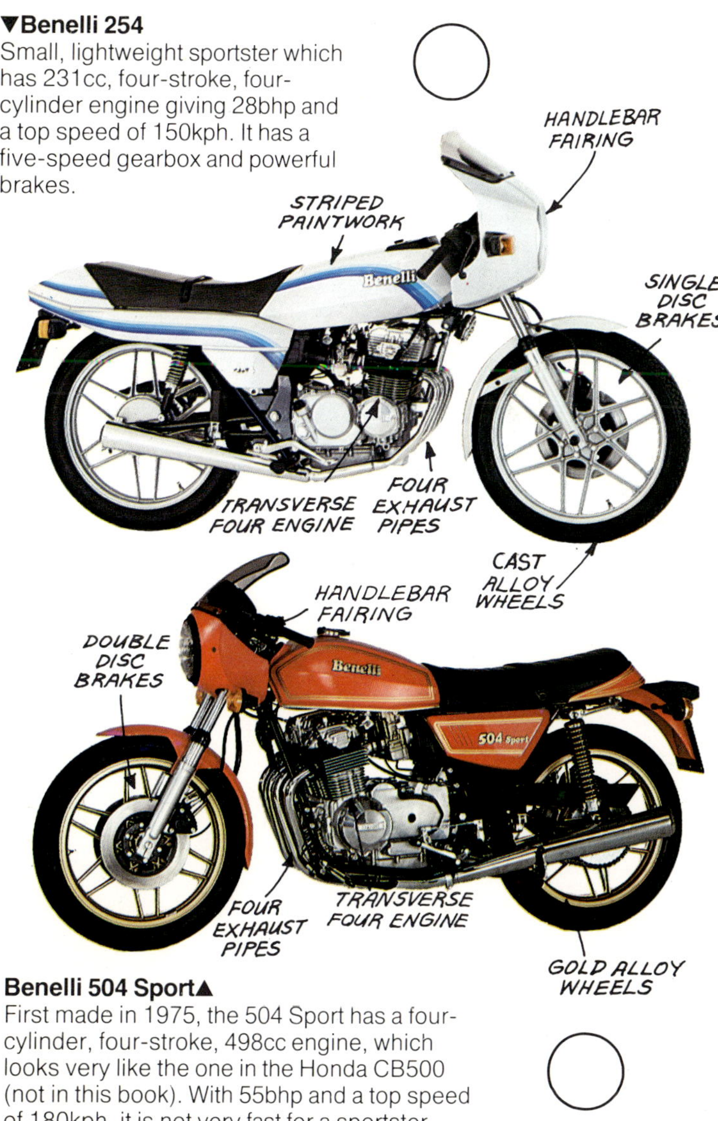

Benelli 504 Sport▲
First made in 1975, the 504 Sport has a four-cylinder, four-stroke, 498cc engine, which looks very like the one in the Honda CB500 (not in this book). With 55bhp and a top speed of 180kph, it is not very fast for a sportster.

Benelli (Italy), BMW (West Germany)

▼Benelli 900 Sei

Developed from the 750 Sei, the world's first commercially built six-cylinder motorbike (*sei* is Italian for six), the 900 is big, wide and very powerful. The 906cc, four-stroke engine gives 80bhp and a top speed of 220kph.

▼BMW R45

The 450cc R45 is the smallest BMW bike. Like all BMWs it is easy to identify by its flat twin-cylinder engine. It has a big fuel tank, which is good for touring, and top speed of 160kph. Do not confuse with the very similar BMW R65.

BMW (West Germany)

BMW R80▼

Very light for its size, the R80 has a 785cc, 55bhp, four-stroke engine and can cruise at 195kph. Look out for the flat twin-cylinder engine, which BMW first used in 1920 and have put in nearly all their bikes since then.

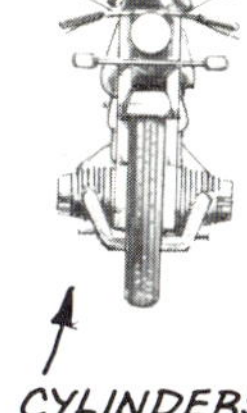

▼BMW R100/RS

One of the biggest and most expensive bikes on the road. It has a 70bhp, 980cc, four-stroke engine and top speed of 210kph. The fairing was specially designed in a wind tunnel to keep the bike stable at high speeds.

BSA* (U.K.)

▼BSA Easy Rider
This 49cc, single-cylinder, two-stroke moped is single speed, or two-speed with an automatic gearbox. The bike frame forms the petrol tank and can hold about 3.5 litres.

BSA 125 Tracker▲
Lightweight trail bike built in Britain, but with a Yamaha 123cc, single-cylinder, two-stroke engine and some Italian parts. With 12bhp and a six-speed gearbox, its top speed is about 115kph.

*The original BSA company collapsed in 1972. The bikes on this page are made by NVT, who bought the famous BSA name for their bikes.

BSA (U.K.), Cagiva (Italy)

BSA Beaver▼

A very small motorbike with a 50cc, single-cylinder, two-stroke engine like a moped's. It has a four-speed gearbox and kick-starter like bigger bikes, but a top speed of only 50kph.

Cagiva SST 250▲

Sportster with single-cylinder, two-stroke, 240cc engine and five-speed gearbox. It has a kick-starter and top speed of 135kph. Look out, too, for the SST 350 sportster which has a bigger engine and top speed of 145kph.

Cagiva (Italy), CZ (Czechoslovakia)

▼Cagiva SX 250
Trail bike with same single-cylinder, two-stroke, 240cc engine and five-speed gearbox as the SST 250. It has a high-level exhaust system and high handlebars. Look out for the SX 350 too.

HIGH HANDLEBARS

HIGH MUDGUARDS

SX 250 BADGE

TRIALS TYRES

CZ 250 Custom▶
Solid, sturdy commuter with 246cc, twin-cylinder, two-stroke engine giving 17bhp. It is not very powerful and has a top speed of only 125kph, but is cheap for its size.

HANDLEBAR FAIRING

CZ BADGE

WIRE SPOKE WHEELS

PARALLEL TWIN ENGINE TILTS FORWARDS

LOOK OUT FOR SMOKY EXHAUST

DKW (West Germany), Ducati (Italy)

▼DKW W2000

This has a special 300cc rotary engine with no pistons. It is smooth and very powerful for a small bike, with a top speed of 170kph and good acceleration.

Ducati Darmah▼

Ducati bikes are famous for speed and good road-holding. The Darmah has an 864cc, 60bhp, V-twin engine and top speed of 195kph. Older models are red, but look out for latest black and gold Darmahs.

DUCATI TIGER BADGE

CURVED SEAT

BIG HEADLAMP

IN-LINE V-TWIN ENGINE

Ducati (Italy), Dunstall (U.K./Japan)

▼Ducati 900 SS
This powerful sportster has the same engine and five-speed gearbox as the Darmah, but is lighter and, with a top speed of 238kph, one of the fastest bikes on the road. It is also very noisy, so listen for the sound of the exhaust.

Dunstall GS 1000 CS▲
This is a Suzuki GS 1000 bike, adapted by a British engineer, Paul Dunstall, to make it faster. Four-cylinder, 997cc engine gives 100bhp and a top speed of 238kph.

Enfield (India), Fantic (Italy)

Enfield 350▼
Old British motorbike, first made in 1949 by Royal Enfield. It is now made in Madras, India, and has hardly changed over the years. Looks like a vintage bike, with big, single-cylinder, four-stroke 346cc, 17bhp engine.

Fantic Caballero▼
Small trail bike with 50cc, two-stroke, single-cylinder engine which gives 7bhp and a top speed of 85kph. It is very light and has powerful brakes, a six-speed gearbox and good suspension. Look out, too, for the competition version, Caballero Casa.

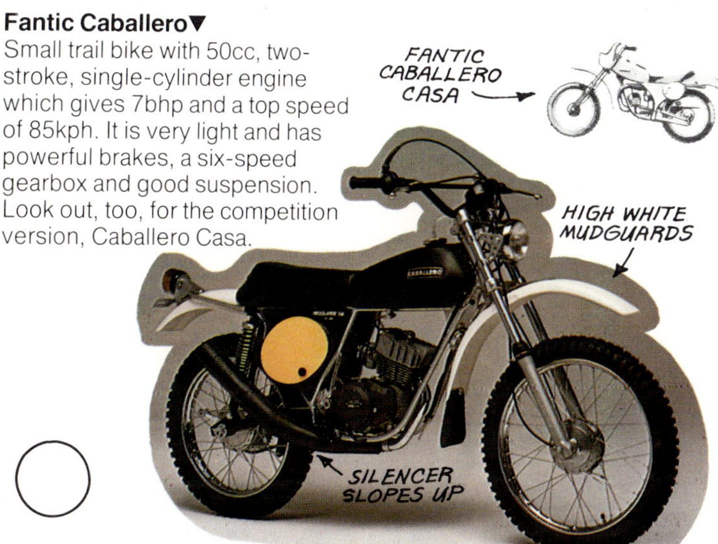

Garelli (Italy), Gilera (Italy)

Garelli KL50▼

The 50 stands for 50kph, the top speed of this small trail bike. It has a 49cc, two-stroke, single-cylinder engine, giving 3bhp, and a five-speed gearbox. Look out for the black handlebars and exhaust pipe.

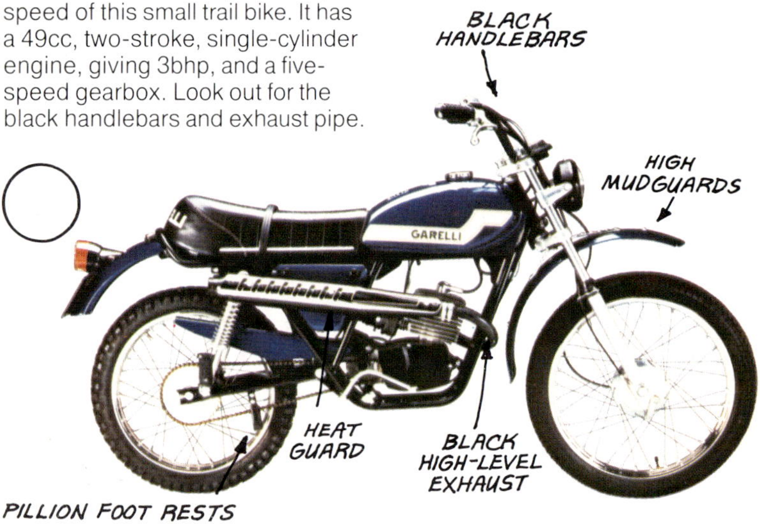

BLACK HANDLEBARS
HIGH MUDGUARDS
HEAT GUARD
BLACK HIGH-LEVEL EXHAUST
PILLION FOOT RESTS

Gilera Trial 50▼

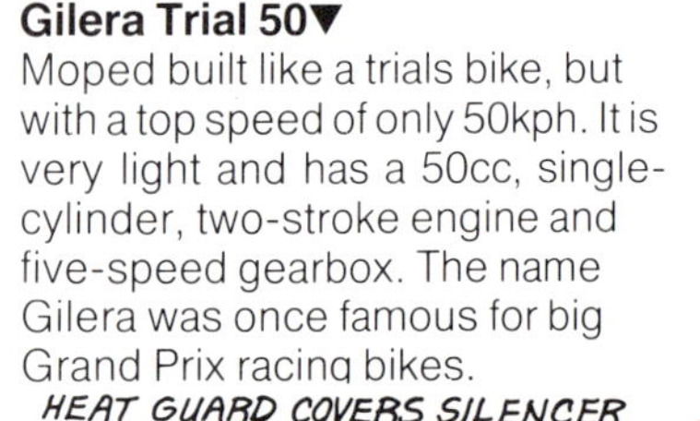

Moped built like a trials bike, but with a top speed of only 50kph. It is very light and has a 50cc, single-cylinder, two-stroke engine and five-speed gearbox. The name Gilera was once famous for big Grand Prix racing bikes.

Harley-Davidson (U.S.A.)

Harley-Davidson XLH-1000 Sportster▼

Big, heavy sportster, made by one of the oldest motorbike makers, who started in 1903 in a shed in Milwaukee, U.S.A. The 997cc, V-twin engine is powerful (61bhp), but the bike is clumsy and not very fast for a sportster.

Harley-Davidson FLH-80* Electra Glide▼

The first Electra Glide was made in 1922 and this enormous cruiser is still used by the American police force. It has a 1339cc, 65bhp, V-twin engine, but weighing 360kg, it can only just reach 170kph.

*80 stands for 80 cubic inches which equals 1339cc and is the size of the engine.

Honda (Japan)

▲Honda NC50 Express
Two-stroke, single-cylinder, 50cc moped giving 2bhp and a top speed of 50kph. It has no gearbox and an unusual starting system with a foot-pedal and spring. Uses very little petrol.

★ LISTEN FOR SOFT, FOUR-STROKE EXHAUST NOISE

CHAIN CASE

LOW STEP-THROUGH FRAME

WIRE-SPOKE WHEELS

◀Honda C70
Lightweight commuter bike based on the 1958, 50cc Honda Cub, the world's best-selling bike. The C70 has a 72cc, 6bhp, single-cylinder engine with a top speed of 76kph and a three-speed gearbox. Look out, too, for the C50 and C90.

Honda (Japan)

▲Honda CB100
Small, 99cc, single-cylinder, four-stroke bike with most of the equipment of the larger Hondas but no electric starter. It has a five-speed gearbox and top speed of 110kph with 10.5bhp.

Honda CG125▼
Single-cylinder commuter with 124cc, four-stroke engine and five-speed gearbox. With about 11bhp, it has a top speed of 110kph. Look out for the case over the chain.

Honda (Japan)

▼Honda XL500S

One of the few four-stroke trail bikes (most are two-stroke). It has a single-cylinder, 498cc, 34bhp engine, but is not as powerful as two-stroke trail bikes. Look out, too, for the XL250 which has a smaller, 248cc, 20bhp engine.

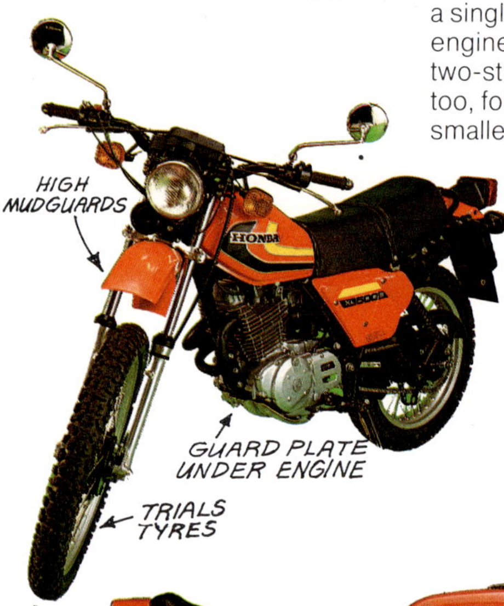

HIGH MUDGUARDS
GUARD PLATE UNDER ENGINE
TRIALS TYRES

TWO EXHAUST PIPES THROUGH MIDDLE OF BIKE

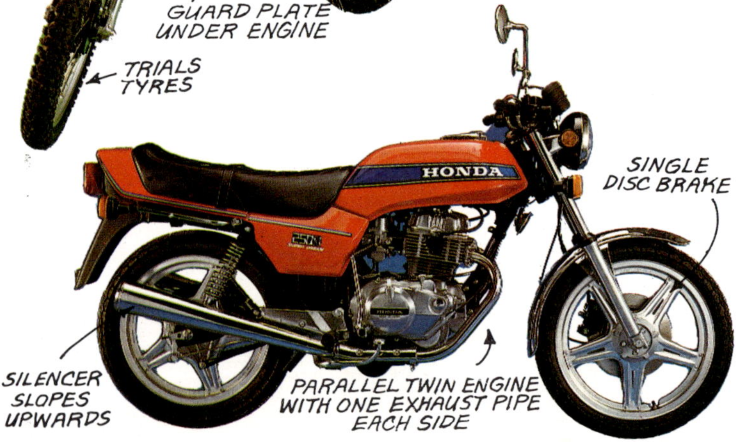

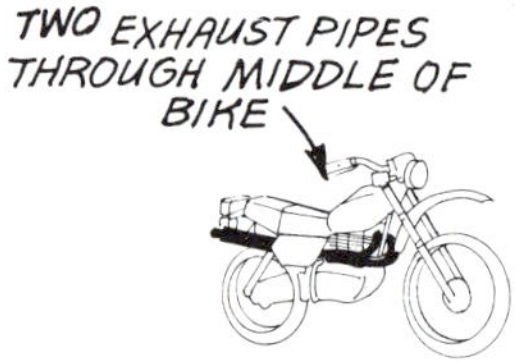

SINGLE DISC BRAKE
SILENCER SLOPES UPWARDS
PARALLEL TWIN ENGINE WITH ONE EXHAUST PIPE EACH SIDE
SPECIAL HONDA WHEELS WITH FLAT METAL SPOKES

Honda CB250N Super Dream▲

Popular, twin-cylinder bike with 249cc, 27bhp, four-stroke engine and six-speed gearbox. Heavy for its engine size, but still quite fast with a top speed of 140kph. Look out, too, for CB400N Super Dream, which has larger engine and double disc brakes.

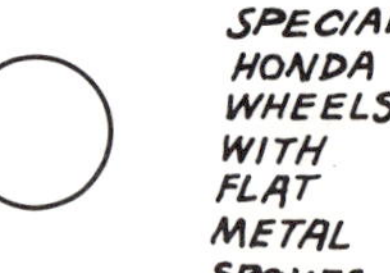

Honda (Japan)

Honda CX500▼

One of Honda's best-selling bikes. It has shaft drive and a 496cc, transverse V-twin engine, giving 50bhp and a top speed of 178kph. With a five-speed gearbox, it is smooth and quiet, stable at high speed and comfortable to ride, so it is good for touring.

Honda CB750KZ▼

Based on the 1968 CB750 Four, which was the first mass-produced road bike to have disc brakes. The CB750KZ has electric starter, disc brakes and a 748cc, 77bhp four-cylinder engine, with a top speed of 215kph.

Honda (Japan)

Honda GL1000 Gold Wing▼

This popular, big tourer is luxurious and comfortable to ride, and very quiet. It has a five-speed gearbox and a 999cc, flat four-cylinder, water-cooled engine, with a top speed of 200kph. Look out for the G L1100 Gold Wing which has black alloy wheels.

Honda CBX▼

Honda's top sportster with a 1047cc, six-cylinder engine. Although heavy and very wide, it has excellent acceleration and a top speed of 238kph. Latest versions have 95bhp and are a bit slower than older models which had 105bhp.

Jawa (Czechoslovakia)

Jawa 350▲
Tough, slow and built to last, this bike is based on the Jawa Senior of the 1950s. It has a four-speed gearbox and twin-cylinder, two-stroke, 343cc engine, giving 28bhp and a top speed of only 140kph.

Jawa Free Wheeler▲
Single-cylinder moped with 49cc, two-stroke engine and automatic, two-speed gearbox. With 26bhp it has a top speed of 50kph.

Kawasaki (Japan)

Kawasaki KC 100▼
One of the best 100cc commuter bikes with powerful brakes and strong suspension. It has single-cylinder, two-stroke engine, five-speed gearbox and is very easy to control. Top speed is 110kph.

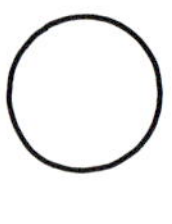

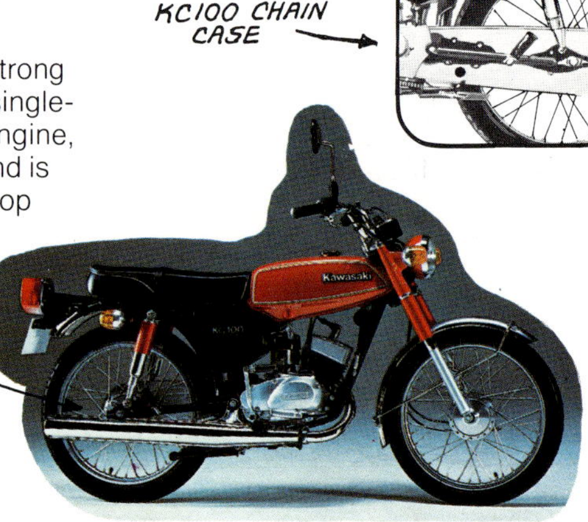

HIGH MUDGUARDS
HIGH-LEVEL EXHAUST SYSTEM
TRIALS TYRES

◀Kawasaki KE 175
One of the very few trail bikes good enough to use in enduro competitions , but not quite as good as its rival, the Yamaha DT 175MX (page 44). It has 174cc, single-cylinder two-stroke engine giving 16 bhp and top speed of 130kph, and a five-speed gearbox.

Kawasaki KH 250▶
This 249cc sportster with three-cylinder, two-stroke engine is the last remaining Kawasaki two-stroke triple. These were incredibly fast and noisy, but hard to control. This KH 250 is less powerful than the old triples and has 28bhp and a top speed of 150kph.

Kawasaki (Japan)

Kawasaki Z200▼

This small, 198cc commuter bike has a single-cylinder, four-stroke engine and five-speed gearbox. With 18bhp, it can cruise at 120kph and uses very little petrol. Look out, too, for the larger Z250C, which has a 246cc engine and top speed of 130kph.

Kawasaki Z650▲

Popular, medium-weight sports tourer with 652cc, four-cylinder, four-stroke engine. With 64bhp and top speed of 195kph, it has good acceleration and is sometimes used for racing. Look out, too, for versions with double disc brakes and cast alloy wheels.

Kawasaki (Japan)

Kawasaki Z1000▲

This superbike's engine has also been used in dragsters, cars, boats and aircraft, and has won lots of speed records. It is a 1015cc, four-stroke transverse four with 90bhp and a top speed of 220kph.

Kawasaki Z1300▲

This gigantic tourer looks clumsy but is very smooth to ride. Its massive 1286cc, six-cylinder engine is water-cooled and it has a five-speed gearbox. With 120bhp, it has a top speed of 230kph, but uses a great deal of petrol.

Lambretta (India), Laverda (Italy)

▼Lambretta 150 GP
Tough, well-built scooter with 148cc, single-cylinder, two-stroke engine and a top speed of 98kph. Lambrettas were first made in Italy in the 1940s, but are now made only in India. Look out, too, for the 200 GP.

Laverda 500 Alpino S▲
This lightweight sportster is fast and easy to control. The six-speed gearbox and 497cc, twin cylinder, four-stroke engine with 48bhp give a top speed of 178kph.

Laverda (Italy)

Laverda Jota▼
Big sportster with 981cc, three-cylinder engine. It requires skill to ride, but is fast and powerful with at least 90bhp and a top speed of 238kph. Developed in Britain from the Italian Laverda 1000, it has strong suspension and powerful brakes.

Laverda Mirage▼
The Mirage is a version of the Laverda 1200 adapted in Britain to make it faster and more sporty. It has a three-cylinder, 1115cc engine, giving 85bhp. Its top speed of 210kph is a bit lower than the Laverda Jota's but it has better acceleration up to 170kph. This version is sold only in Britain.

Moto-Guzzi (Italy)

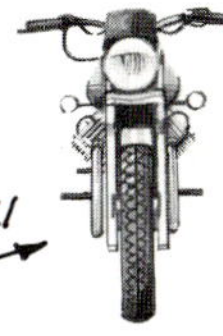

Moto-Guzzi V50▼
This bike with a 490cc, transverse V-twin engine and five-speed gearbox is small but powerful. It is lighter than a lot of the Japanese 250s, and with 39bhp has a top speed of 170kph.

Moto-Guzzi 850 Le Mans▼
This sportster's engine was originally made for an army trike. It is an 844cc, 75bhp, four-stroke transverse V-twin and gives the bike a top speed of 220kph. This is the fastest Moto-Guzzi and it holds the road well.

Moto-Guzzi (Italy), Moto Morini (Italy)

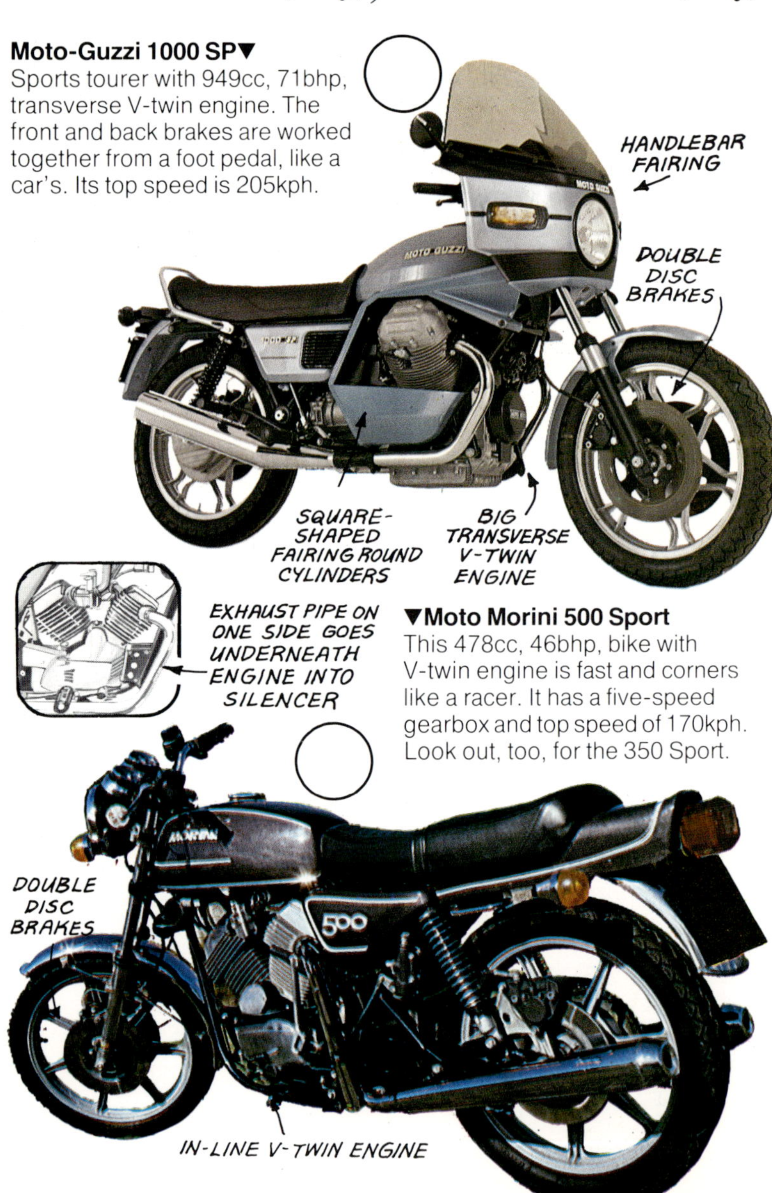

Moto-Guzzi 1000 SP▼
Sports tourer with 949cc, 71bhp, transverse V-twin engine. The front and back brakes are worked together from a foot pedal, like a car's. Its top speed is 205kph.

▼Moto Morini 500 Sport
This 478cc, 46bhp, bike with V-twin engine is fast and corners like a racer. It has a five-speed gearbox and top speed of 170kph. Look out, too, for the 350 Sport.

MZ (East Germany)

▼MZ TS 150

Unusual looking bike, but tough, sturdy and cheap. It has a single-cylinder, two-stroke 143cc engine and four-speed gearbox. Look out too, for the TS 125 which has a 123cc engine.

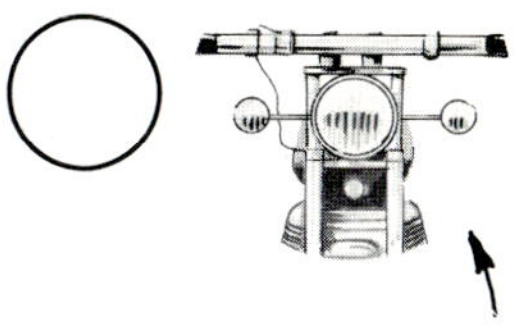

MZ TS 250 Supa 5▼

Tourer with 243cc, single-cylinder two-stroke engine which is mounted on rubber. It has a five-speed gearbox and although it has only 21bhp, can cruise smoothly at 135kph.

Neval (U.S.S.R.)

Neval 125 Electronic▼
Like most other motorbikes from Eastern Europe, the Neval is strongly-built, but not very up-to-date, and the electronic ignition is added by the importers. The 123cc, single-cylinder, two-stroke engine gives 12.5bhp and top speed of 85khp.

Neval Dnieper▼
Old-fashioned looking, but very tough bike, which usually has a sidecar attached. The 650cc engine is a flat twin, and it has a four-speed gearbox and top speed of 100kph with sidecar. There is a 750cc version too, which has a reverse gear.

Puch (Austria)

Puch Maxi and Maxi Executive
Both these mopeds have 2bhp, 49cc single-cylinder, two-stroke engines. The Maxi is single- or two-speed and the Maxi Executive is two-speed with an automatic gearbox.

Sanglas (Spain), Silk (U.K.)

▼Sanglas 500-S2

This big, single-cylinder bike has a 500cc, 35bhp engine, five-speed gearbox and electric starter. Its top speed is 160kph. It is made in a small factory in Spain and ridden by the Spanish police force.

Silk 700S▲

This rare bike is hand-built to order and named after the man who makes them. Its 650cc engine is a larger, modern version of an old Scott* water-cooled, two-stroke twin. It has a four-speed gearbox and top speed of 178kph.

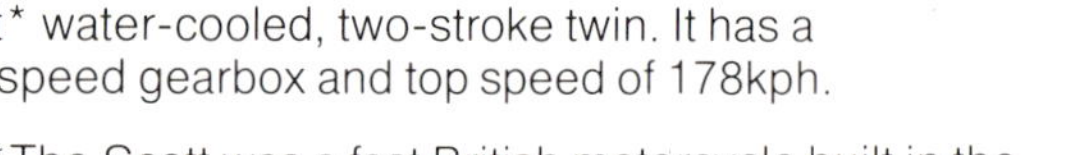

*The Scott was a fast British motorcycle built in the 1920s and 30s.

Suzuki (Japan)

Suzuki FS50 Snip▼
Moped which looks like a scooter. It has small wheels and a 49cc, two-stroke, single-cylinder engine and automatic two-speed gearbox.

Suzuki ZR50X1▲
This moped looks like a motorbike, but has only a 49cc, single-cylinder, two-stroke engine and five-speed gearbox. With 3bhp it has a top speed of 50kph.

Suzuki (Japan)

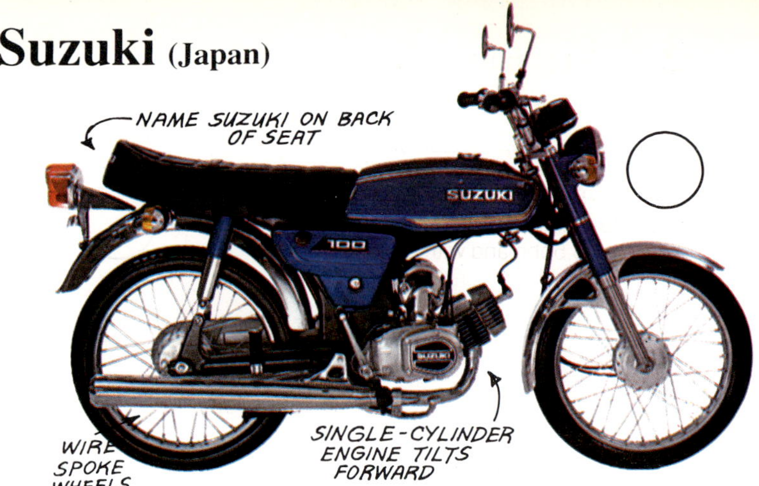

Suzuki A100▲

Suzuki's smallest motorbike with 98cc, 9.5bhp, single-cylinder, two-stroke engine and four-speed gearbox. It is a commuter, but is very lightweight and has a top speed of 100kph.

Suzuki GP125▲

This has a 123cc, single-cylinder, two-stroke engine which is quite powerful, giving 15bhp, and a five-speed gearbox. Its top speed is 125kph, and it is a little larger than the A100.

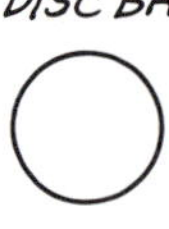

Suzuki (Japan)

Suzuki TS185▼

This trail bike is one of the best for off-road riding and rivals the Yamaha DT 175MX (page 44). Its 183cc, single-cylinder, two-stroke engine gives 16.5bhp and with a five-speed gearbox, top speed is 130kph.

HEAT GUARD

HIGH MUDGUARD

BLACK HIGH-LEVEL EXHAUST SYSTEM

Suzuki GT250X7▼

This is the latest version of the GT250, first brought out in 1967. It is a 247cc, 30bhp sportster and is faster than most 250s and some 500s. It has a twin-cylinder, two-stroke engine and six-speed gearbox.

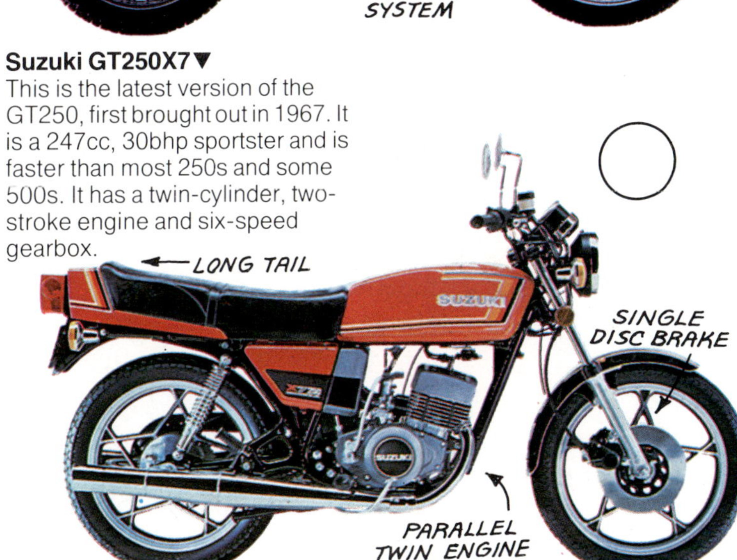

Suzuki (Japan)

Suzuki GN400▼
This 396cc tourer has a big, single-cylinder, four-stroke engine, which is unusual for a Japanese bike. It has a five-speed gearbox.

◀Suzuki GS425
A sporty tourer with a 423cc, four-stroke, twin-cylinder engine and six-speed gearbox. With 40bhp and top speed of 170kph, it is the fastest of all the Japanese medium-weight twins.

Suzuki (Japan)

▼Suzuki GS550

This 549cc sportster is one of the fastest 500s on sale. Its four-cylinder, four-stroke engine with six-speed gearbox gives a top speed of 195kph. It is quite small, but has very powerful brakes.

▼Suzuki GS750

Suzuki first made this big, four-cylinder bike in 1977 and it is now thought to be one of the world's best. The 747cc, four-stroke engine gives 68bhp and a top speed of 210kph. It is stable and corners well at high speed.

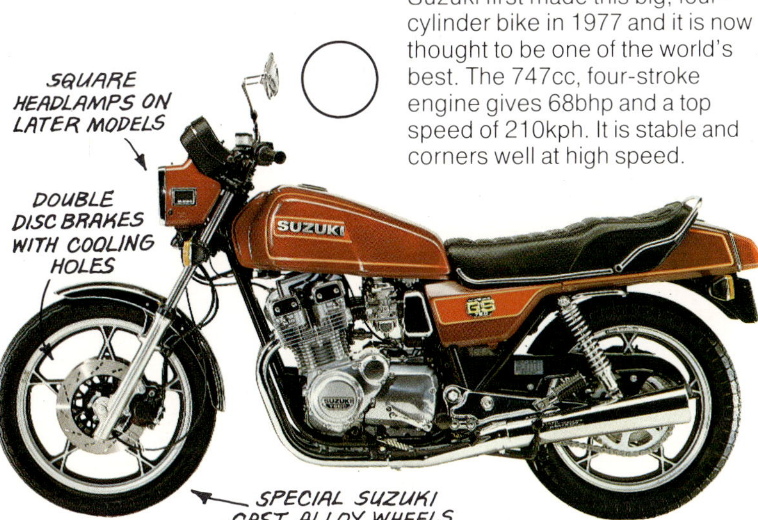

Suzuki (Japan)

▼Suzuki GS850
Big tourer similar to the GS750, but with a larger, 843cc, 80bhp engine and shaft drive. It is built to travel long distances at high speed and is comfortable to ride.

Suzuki GSX1100▼
Fastest Japanese bike on sale. Its four-cylinder, four-stroke, 1075cc engine gives 104bhp and a top speed of 245kph. It is as light as most 750s and is enormously powerful with excellent acceleration.

Triumph (U.K.), Vespa (Italy)

▼Triumph Bonneville T140
This 744cc parallel twin is a larger, more modern version of the 1937 Triumph Speed Twin, the most widely copied bike in motorcycle history. With only 54bhp, it has a top speed of 190kph and is stable at high speed.

FORK COVERS

LISTEN FOR LOW, THROATY EXHAUST NOISE

✱WATCH FOR BIKE BEING KICK-STARTED AS NO ELECTRIC STARTER

PARALLEL TWIN ENGINE WITH ONE EXHAUST PIPE EACH SIDE

SINGLE DISC BRAKE

▼Vespa Bravo
Moped with 50cc, single-cylinder, two-stroke engine and strong suspension. Its top speed is 50kph. Vespa are owned by Piaggio, so look out for the Piaggio badge.

HIGH HANDLEBARS

PETROL TANK

LOOK OUT FOR PIAGGIO BADGE ON VESPA BIKES.

FLAT, SINGLE-CYLINDER ENGINE

WIRE SPOKE WHEELS

Vespa (Italy)

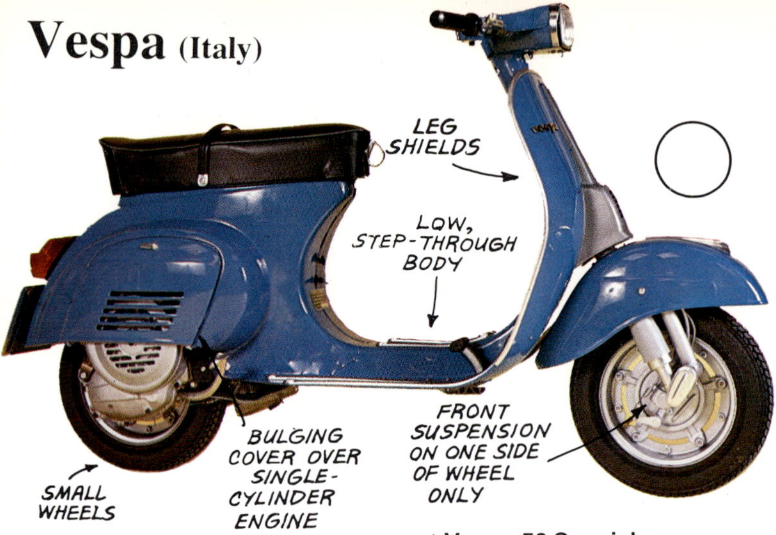

▲Vespa 50 Special
Moped built like a small scooter, with 1.5bhp, two-stroke, single-cylinder 50cc engine, three gears and a top speed of 50kph.

▲Vespa P200
This scooter has a 198cc, single-cylinder, two-stroke engine and four-speed gearbox on one side of the back wheel, and a spare wheel on the other side. Top speed is 120kph and it is very quiet. Piaggio invented the modern scooter in 1946.

Yamaha (Japan)

◀Yamaha FS1
Very popular moped nicknamed "Fizzy" It has a single-cylinder, two-stroke, 49cc engine, four-speed gearbox and front disc or drum brakes.

Yamaha RD 50▶
Classed as a moped, with a 49cc, single-cylinder, two-stroke engine. Looks more like a motorbike than the FS1 and has a five-speed gearbox and better acceleration.

SINGLE DISC BRAKE

WIRE SPOKE WHEELS

◀Yamaha RS 125
Very small motorbike with 123cc, two-stroke single-cylinder engine and five-speed gearbox. Its top speed is 125kph. Look out, too, for the RS 100.which has a smaller, 97cc engine and top speed of 115kph.

Yamaha (Japan)

▼Yamaha RD 125
This fast, lightweight and sporty bike is based on the 1968 Yamaha 98cc AS1. With a 124cc, two-stroke twin engine, it has good acceleration and a top speed of 125kph. Look out, too, for the similar 198cc RD 200.

Yamaha DT 175MX▲
Popular trail bike, good enough for enduro competitions*. It has single-cylinder, 171cc, two-stroke engine and top speed of 115kph. With 16bhp, it is less powerful than many trail bikes, but light and very tough.

 *For more about enduro competitions see page 51.

Yamaha (Japan)

Yamaha RD 400▼

One of the best two-stroke bikes ever made. It has a 398cc, 43bhp, two-cylinder engine with good acceleration and top speed of 180kph. Powerful and stable at high speeds, it was developed from the same bike as the old Yamaha Grand Prix racers.

LOOKS VERY LIKE RD 250 BUT HAS "400" ON SIDE COVER

SINGLE DISC BRAKE

BLACK PARALLEL TWIN ENGINE TILTS FORWARD

Yamaha RD 350LC▼

Sportster with a top speed of over 205kph, based on the design of the modern Grand Prix racers. Engine is a water-cooled, 347cc, 47bhp, two-stroke parallel twin. (LC stands for "liquid-cooled".)

Yamaha (Japan)

Yamaha XS 250▲

This 248cc, 27bhp, twin-cylinder bike with six-speed gearbox is a bit heavy for its engine size and has a top speed of only 145kph. Look out, too, for the XS 400 which weighs about the same, but goes better with 392cc, 38bhp engine.

▲Yamaha XT 500

Trail bike with big, single-cylinder, 499cc, 30bhp engine and top speed of 145kph. Single-cylinder engines were very popular on British bikes of the 1940s and 50s, and Yamaha was the first Japanese company to use them on modern bikes.

Yamaha (Japan)

Yamaha XS 500▲
This bike was first made in 1974 and has a 498cc, 48bhp, four-stroke, twin-cylinder engine and five-speed gearbox. Top speed is 185kph.

▼Yamaha XS 650 Special
First made in 1970, the XS 650 has a four-stroke, parallel twin engine, very like the one in the Triumph Bonneville (page 41). With 654cc and 50bhp its top speed is 178kph. The Special has high American-style handlebars, but look out, too, for the tourer version with lower handlebars.

HIGH HANDLEBARS

"US CUSTOM" BADGE

SINGLE DISC BRAKE

PARALLEL TWIN ENGINE

Yamaha (Japan)

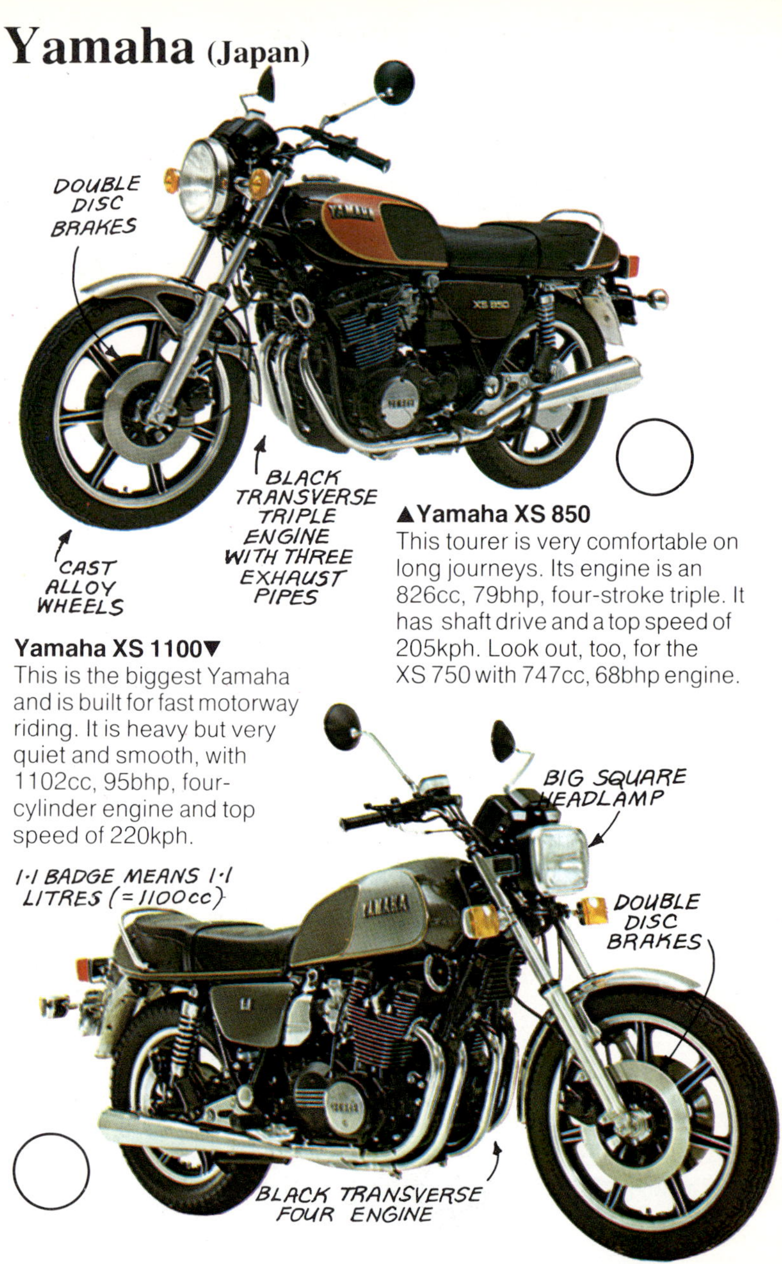

▲Yamaha XS 850
This tourer is very comfortable on long journeys. Its engine is an 826cc, 79bhp, four-stroke triple. It has shaft drive and a top speed of 205kph. Look out, too, for the XS 750 with 747cc, 68bhp engine.

Yamaha XS 1100▼
This is the biggest Yamaha and is built for fast motorway riding. It is heavy but very quiet and smooth, with 1102cc, 95bhp, four-cylinder engine and top speed of 220kph.

Motorbike accessories

Some motorcyclists fit special handlebars, seats, fairings and other accessories to their bikes. Watch out for these when you are bike spotting, as they can make it hard to recognize the shape of the bike. Here are some of the things you may see.

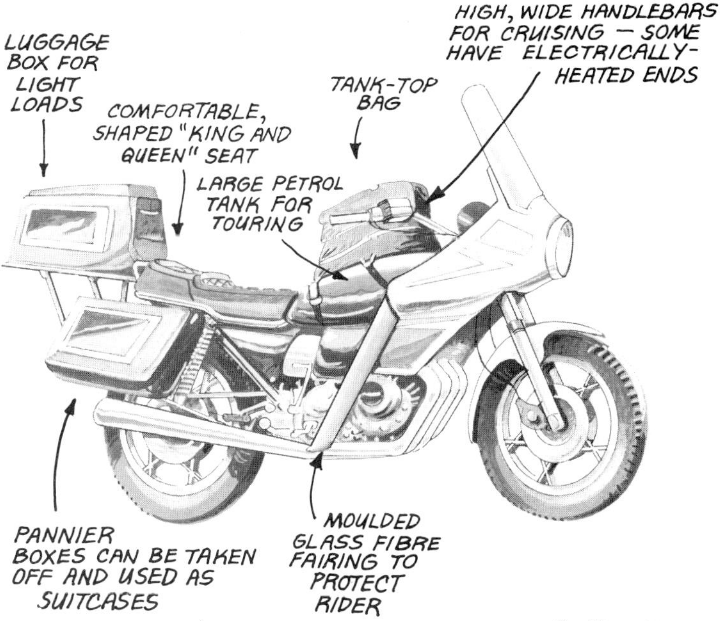

HIGH, WIDE HANDLEBARS FOR CRUISING — SOME HAVE ELECTRICALLY-HEATED ENDS

LUGGAGE BOX FOR LIGHT LOADS

TANK-TOP BAG

COMFORTABLE, SHAPED "KING AND QUEEN" SEAT

LARGE PETROL TANK FOR TOURING

PANNIER BOXES CAN BE TAKEN OFF AND USED AS SUITCASES

MOULDED GLASS FIBRE FAIRING TO PROTECT RIDER

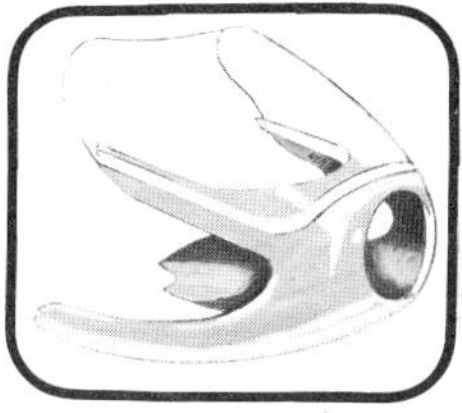

Handlebar fairing

Small fairing and windscreen which fits round the headlamp.

Racing seat

Short, low seat with back-stop to support rider in racing position.

Racing handlebars

Low, narrow handlebars so the rider sits in a low, racing position.

Racing and off-road bikes

Trials

Moto-cross

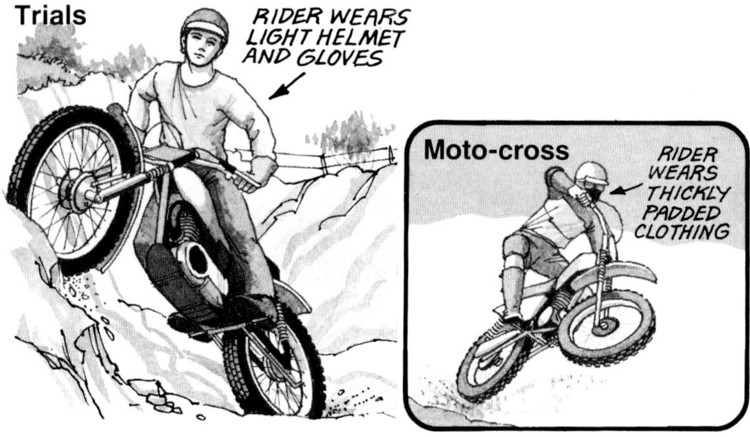

Trials are tests of skill and bike control over a very rough and hazardous course. The riders must not touch the ground with their feet, and it is the competitor with the least faults, not the fastest, who wins.

This is a fast race over a rough, cross-country course. The circuit is usually about ten laps round a 1.5km course and the rider with the fastest time wins.

Trials bikes

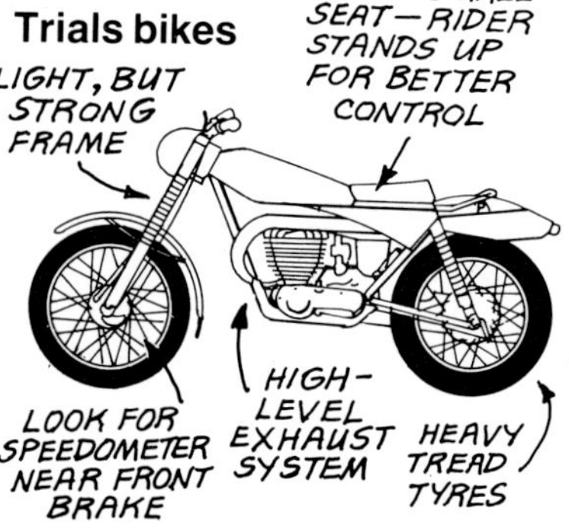

These are light and high off the ground and built to keep going at low speeds. Engine size is usually about 250cc, giving 14bhp.

Moto-cross bikes

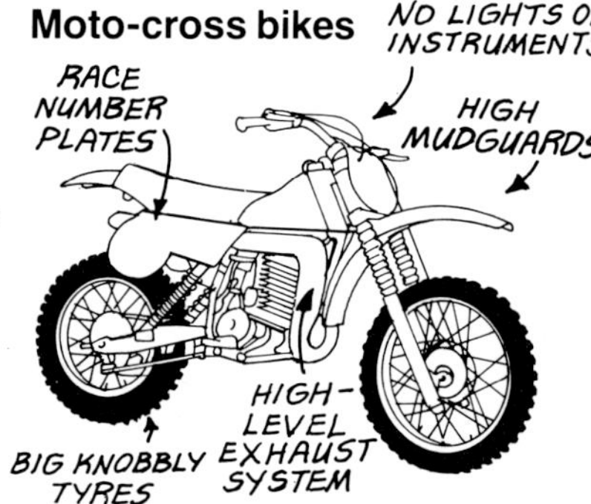

These have a very strong frame and a fast, road-racing type engine which can reach speeds of 160kph with 50bhp. The tyres have huge knobbles on them.

Drag races

In these, each racer tries to cover a quarter of a mile (424m) in the shortest time from a standing start. The best American drag racers can do this in about 7.5 seconds, reaching speeds of 339kph.

The huge, 2000cc or more engines run on nitro-methanol, which is much more powerful than petrol. Some racers even set the track on fire to melt the back tyre and give it a better grip.

Enduros

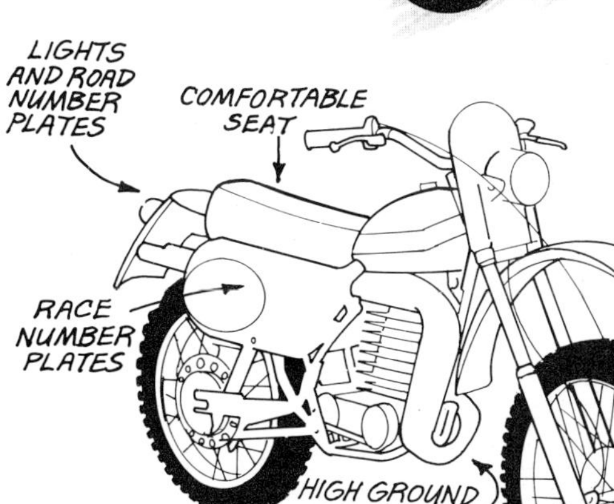

These bikes are built for very long distance races over rough and rugged country. They have the frame and suspension of a trials bike, and an engine with plenty of power. The most famous enduro competition is the Internationl Six Days Trial.

Road races

Nowadays, most road races are held on special tracks, and only the Isle of Man Tourist Trophy is still held on public roads. International championship road races are called Grand Prix. The bikes have top speeds of around 300kph and power output of up to 120bhp.

Road racing bike

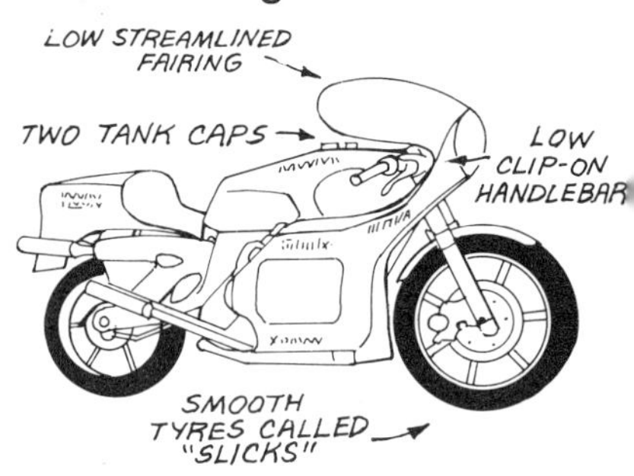

Speedway

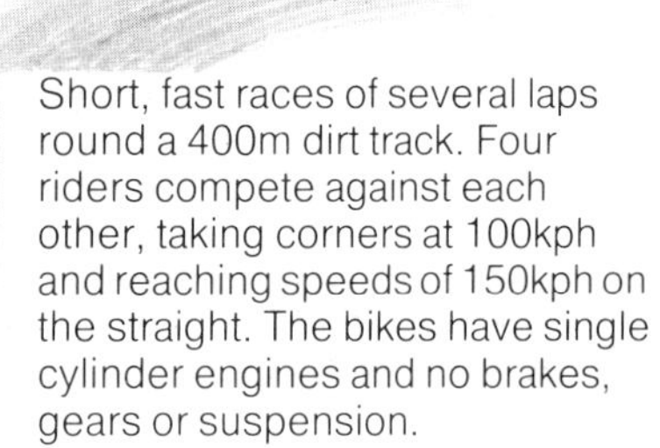

Short, fast races of several laps round a 400m dirt track. Four riders compete against each other, taking corners at 100kph and reaching speeds of 150kph on the straight. The bikes have single cylinder engines and no brakes, gears or suspension.

Bike stunts and records

Doing a wheelie

Stunt rider Dave Taylor did a wheelie (riding on back wheel) for 64km round the Isle of Man Tourist Trophy track.

Most people on a bike

The largest number of people to ride on one motorbike is 17.

Record jump

In 1979, Eddie Kidd jumped over 14 double-decker buses – a distance of 63m. He beat the record set by Evel Knievel who jumped 39m over 19 cars.

Longest bike

This is the Böhmerland. It is over three metres long, with space for three people.

Smallest bike

This bike, made by Kirk Wright of Arizona, U.S.A. has a wheelbase of only 20cm.

Fastest

Don Vesco, in his Kawasaki Lightning Bolt, holds the world speed record for motorcyclists. In 1978, on the Bonneville Salt Flats, U.S.A. he reached a speed of 512.733kph.

Noisiest

A 1935 DKW bike with a megaphone exhaust system was so loud it could be heard all round the Isle of Man course.

Strange bikes

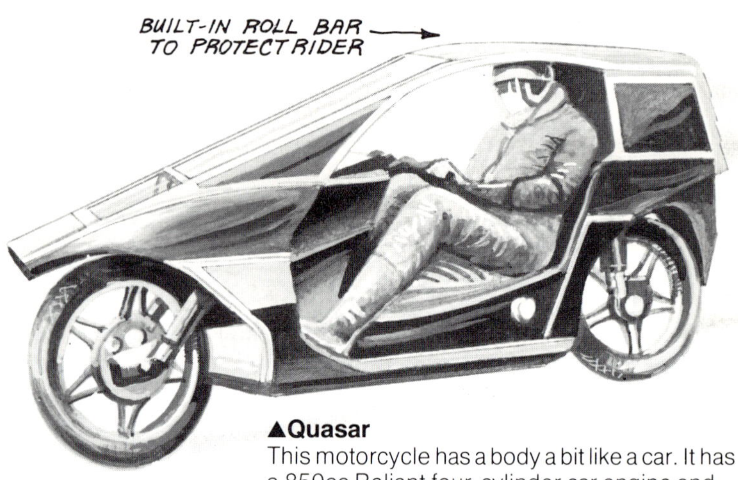

▲Quasar
This motorcycle has a body a bit like a car. It has a 850cc Reliant four-cylinder car engine and the rider sits in a car seat, using car-type controls. With its very streamlined shape, its top speed is 160kph.

▲Triking
This three-wheeler is classed as a sidecar as it weighs less than 355kg. It has two wheels at the front and one at the back, and a windscreen and steering wheel like a car. It can carry one passenger beside the rider. The engine is a 949cc Moto-Guzzi V-twin which gives 70bhp and a top speed of 170kph.

▲Stimson Scorcher

This peculiar machine is a three-wheeled motorbike. The makers supply only the chassis and the owner has to find and install the engine and gearbox – usually those of a Mini. It can carry two passengers behind the rider and has a top speed of between 90kph and 120kph, depending on the engine size.

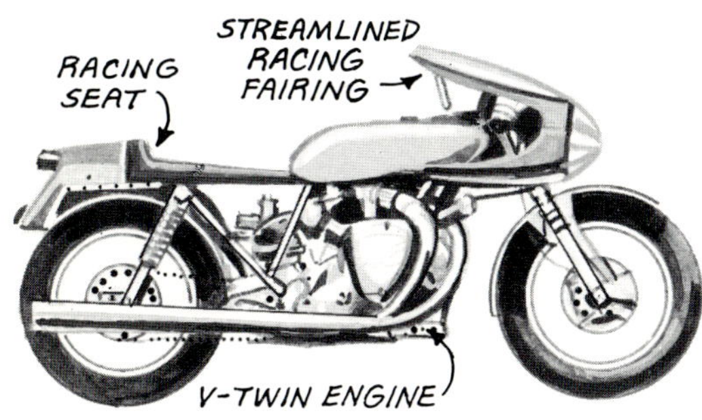

◀Egli-Vincent

These bikes have 998cc V-twin engines from the famous old British Vincent motorcycles. They are rebuilt by Fritz Egli, a Swiss motor-cycle engineer, and fitted into modern racing frames. Egli tunes the engines to give 80bhp and a top speed of 237kph.

Shifty▶

This motorcycle has the engine, gearbox, clutch, radiator and instrument panel from a Fiat 127 car. The 906cc four-cylinder engine gives 53bhp. Ridden with a sidecar the top speed is 150kph, and solo, 186kph.

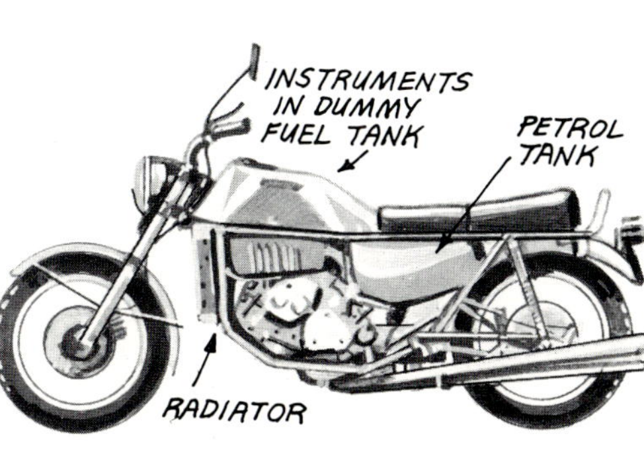

History of the motorbike

The first motorbikes were made in the 1860s by fitting steam engines to bicycles. This one, made in 1884 by Copeland, an American, could reach a speed of 20kph.

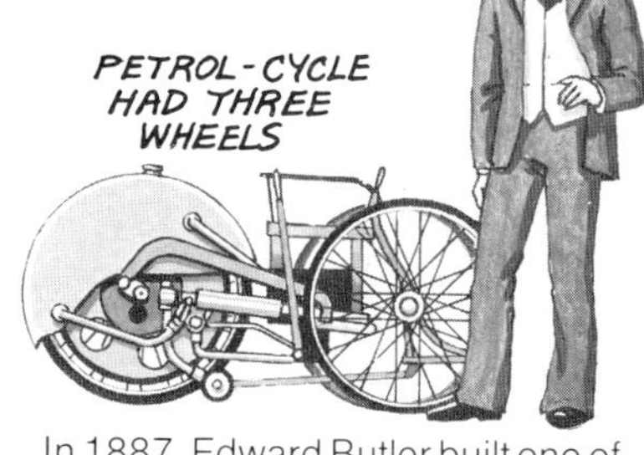

In 1887, Edward Butler built one of the first petrol-engined motor-cycles. It had a two-stroke engine with two cylinders, one either side of the back wheel.

In Paris in 1901, two Russian brothers put the engine low down between the wheels to make their bike, called the "New Werner" more stable.

The 1908 Zenith Gradua had a special system, a bit like gears, to make the engine turn faster when climbing hills. It had a top speed of over 100kph.

Racing was a good way of testing new motorbikes. In 1907 there was the first Tourist Trophy race on the Isle of Man. It was held there to avoid the British speed limit of 33kph.

Modern type telescopic front forks first appeared on the BMW R72 in 1935.

The largest sidecar ever made was the Canterbury Carmobile three-seater.

The first sidecars were made of wicker, to keep them as light as possible. They were very popular until the 1960s, when small cars took over. Some sidecars were big enough to carry three people, with two rows of seats and a boot.

The 650cc Triumph Thunderbird was the first bike to have a modern alternator to produce electricity for the lights, instead of the old dynamo.

In 1968, Honda produced the CB750 Four – the first bike with hydraulic disc brakes. These are much more powerful than the old drum brakes.

Look out for old 1950s bikes on the road, such as this Italian 500cc Moto-Guzzi Falcone, which is now being produced again in Britain.

It has a flat single-cylinder engine and a top speed of 127kph. Look out, too, for the Egli-Vincent (page 55) and other rebuilt machines.

Speedway game

To find out which rider wins the speedway, follow the lines for four laps round the track. If you get lost, the answer is at the bottom of page 64.

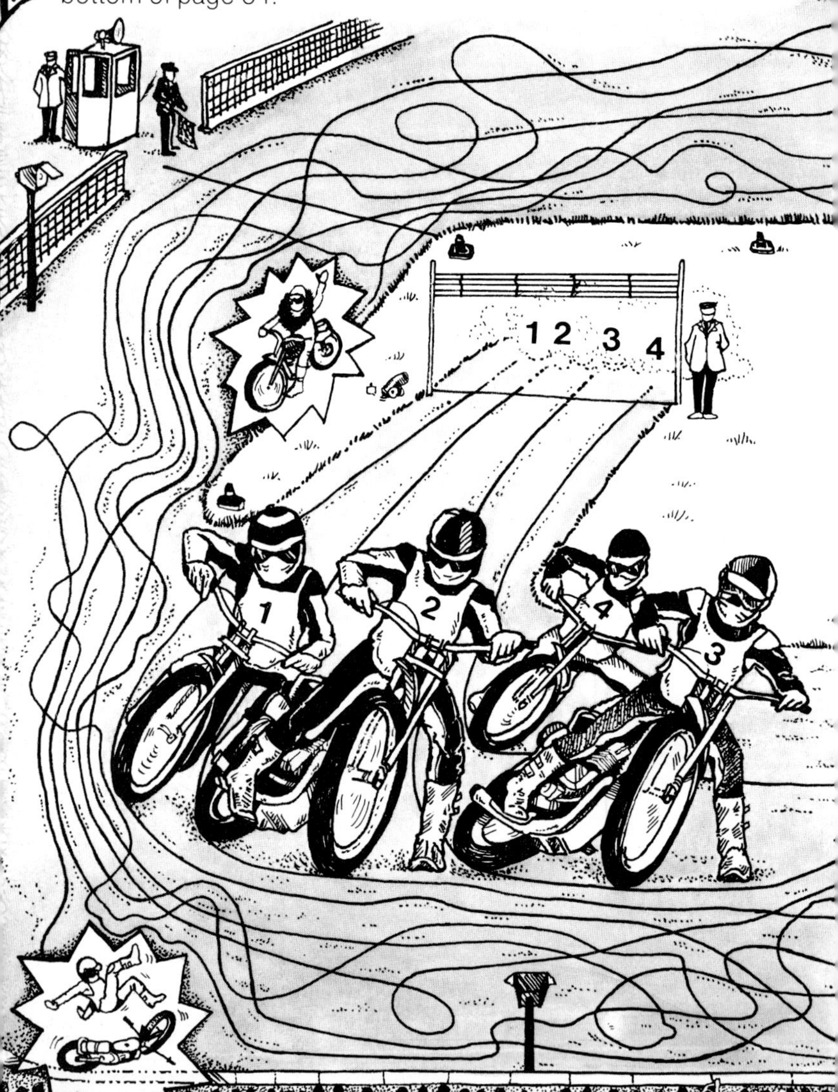

Name the bikes game

Can you recognize these motorbikes? To identify them, look at the mudguards, engines, handlebars and fairings. They are all in this book, but if you get stuck, the answers are at the bottom of the page.

Answers: 1. BMW R80; 2. Vespa P200; 3. Ducati 900 SS; 4. Triumph Bonneville T140; 5. Moto-Guzzi 850 Le Mans; 6. Harley-Davidson FLH-80 Electra Glide; 7. Puch Maxi; 8. Kawasaki Z200; 9. Honda NC50 Express; 10. Yamaha RD400.

Scorecard

On this scorecard you can keep a record of all the motorbikes you see. Each time you spot a bike, write the date in the date column, then, after a day out spotting, you can add up your score. The bikes are arranged in alphabetical order, according to the name of the manufacturer.

Motorbike	Score	Date	Motorbike	Score	Date
AJS FB Ajay	25		Fantic Caballero Casa	20	
Batavus Starglo	10		Garelli KL50	15	
Benelli 254	25		Gilera Trial 50	15	
Benelli 504 Sport	15		Harley-Davidson XLH-1000 Sportster	20	
Benelli 900 Sei	15		Harley-Davidson FLH-80 Electra Glide	20	
BMW R45	10		Honda NC50 Express	5	
BMW R80	10		Honda C70	5	
BMW R100/RS	10		Honda CB100	5	
BSA Easy Rider	10		Honda CG125	5	
BSA 125 Tracker	15		Honda XL500S	10	
BSA Beaver	15		Honda CB250N Super Dream	5	
Cagiva SST 250	15		Honda CX500	5	
Cagiva SX 250	15		Honda CB750KZ	5	
CZ 250 Custom	5		Honda GL1000 Gold Wing	5	
DKW W2000	25		Honda CBX	10	
Ducati Darmah	10		Jawa 350	5	
Ducati 900 SS	15		Jawa Free Wheeler	10	
Dunstall GS 1000 CS	25		Kawasaki KC 100	5	
Enfield 350	20		Kawasaki KE 175	5	
Fantic Caballero	15		Kawasaki KH 250	5	